Once Upon a Page

A guided journal that unlocks different corners of your creativity

By Zee Ladak

Copyright © 2019 by Zee Ladak
Art and Design by Zee Ladak

All right reserved.

No portion of this book may be reproduced, distributed or transmitted in any form or by any means, including photocopying, recording or other electronic or mechanical methods, without the prior written permission of the publisher.

Published and printed in United States

First Printing, 2019

ISBN # 9781695372566

Acknowledgement

This book was made possible with the help of my family and their continued support and motivation. A shout-out to my three kids who are brimming with creativity and who rock my world. Some of Aliya's ideas ended up in this book!
Thanks to the talented artists who have inspired me during the process of this book.

Above all (I leave the best for last) special thanks to the Greatness of the Universe and to You for making this book come to life.

When you own
Once Upon a Page

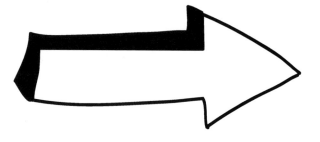

Start from any page - no order

Carry with you everywhere

Embellish as much as possible

Do it with a friend

Outlet for ideas, emotions..

Ignore perfection and get messy

A page a day or more

Share your creativeness

Be adventurous

Cover with colors

MEASURE

the thickness of
of this book without
your creative work

_____ cm.

_____ inches

Entry into my world

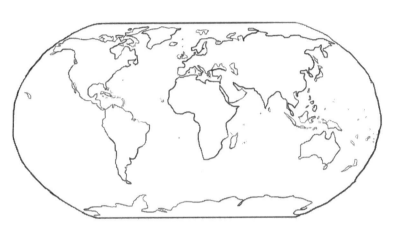

Me: _____

My location: _____

My Neighbor: _____
On my right

My Neighbor: _____
On my left

Write "Hello" in Different Languages

_____

_____

_____

_____

NEWSPAPER AS

Glue newspaper on this spread and

MY CANVAS

create your masterpiece

This page is dedicated to the letter Z

write..
words that begin with

Punch Holes

Take a RIBBON and WEAVE IT

LOOK in the MIRROR and DRAW what you SEE

Pretty amazing huh!

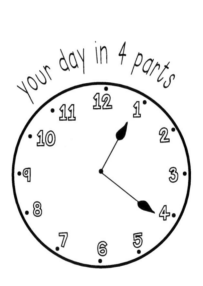

Document time passing

school/work	time with family
DAY	
time for spiritual growth	time for fun

design jewelry using your birthstone

what is your birthstone

Open the MAP

Pick a place you have NEVER been

Why would you want to visit this place?

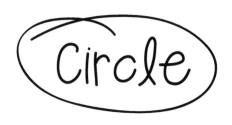

all the **"the"** in this article

What might happen if you stop resisting your heart's desires. What might happen if you had the courage to walk forward towards whatever is whispering to you, whatever is tugging at your heart. What would happen if you stopped telling yourself on repeat that you aren't good enough or it wasn't possible or you don't deserve it. Was there a moment when joy brought you tears of relief? Was there a moment when something cracked open within you? Hold on to that. There is wisdom there. There is truth there.

We need to start somewhere because that's the only way you are gonna get clarity on where you need to pivot, so you can get to the place where you gonna serve the world the most. And of course there is going to be a ton of fear when you go ahead and make the first draft, the beta version of whatever you are making because you think if I am gonna write a script it's gonna be Oscar worthy the first time.

Let go of the need for perfectionism. Let go of that fear that it's not going to be good enough. Brene Brown says, "Perfectionism is a twenty ton shield that we lug around thinking it will protect us when in fact it's the thing that's really preventing us from taking flight.

Perfectionism is a self destructive and addictive believe that fuels this primary thought; if I look perfect and do everything perfectly I can avoid or minimize the painful feeling of shame, judgement and blame"
.
Give yourself permission to just get started!

Excerpts from Don't keep your day job podcast by Cathy Heller
12/31/2018

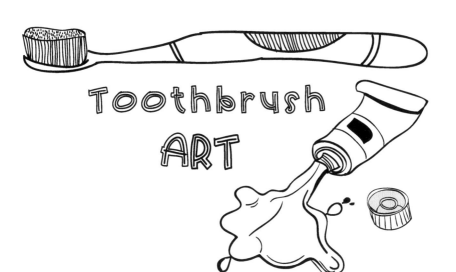

Stick your apparel tags here

Spending

MAKING
the world a little brighter today

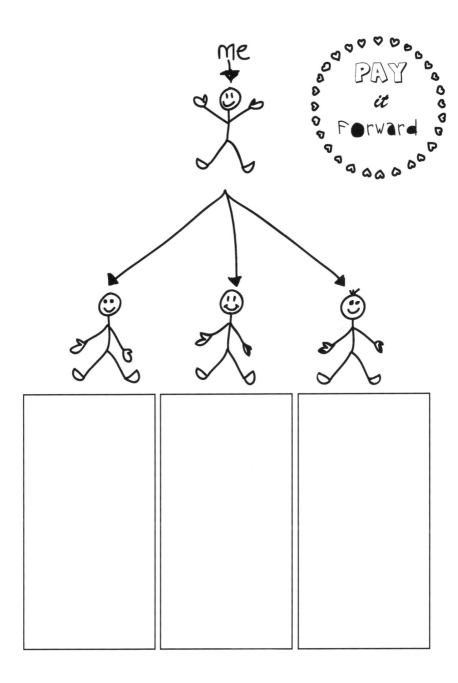

Infuse this page with scent

 and

EMOTIONS

shred it → burn it → store it

Expand the drawing

A one point perspective view

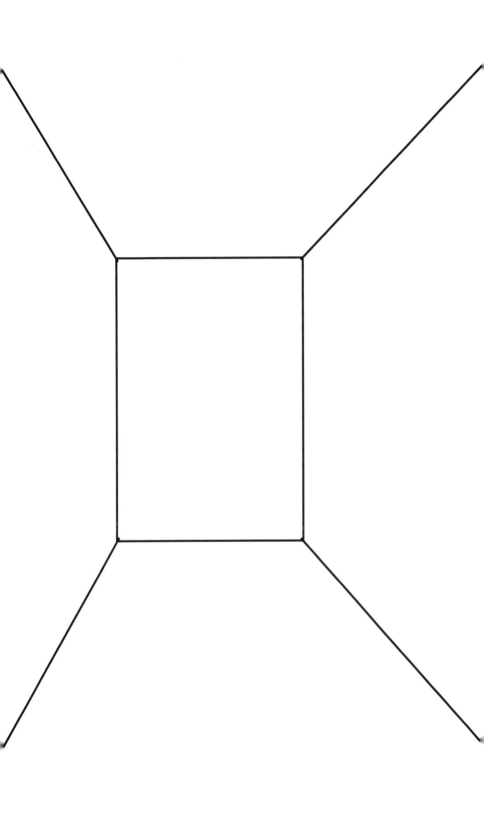

Use

to fill in the doodle shapes

Feel good Songs

Look outside ✲ Look up ✲ Draw what you see

Make Rice Paper

draw ROADS and BRIDGES

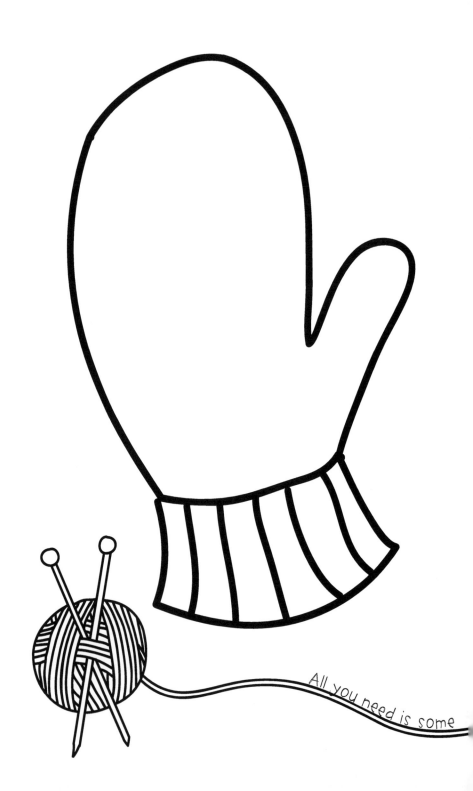

Eat out

Write down possible ingredients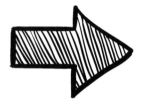

re - CREATE and rename the RECIPE when you get home

Ingredients:

Create

Make your own

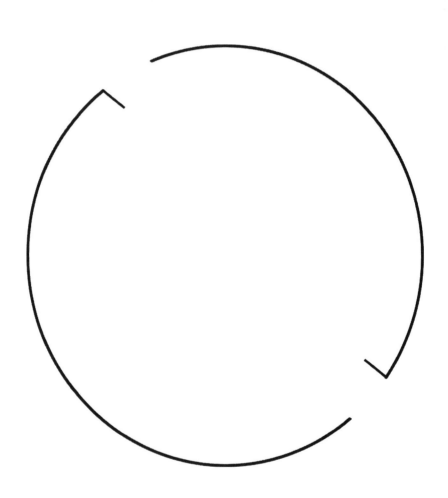

Write your name in **DIFFERENT**

Fonts

Turn a peice of household item into an

Now you try!

A DOZEN DIFFERENT

APPLES

USE DRAPING TO MAKE ONE-OF-A-KIND PIECE

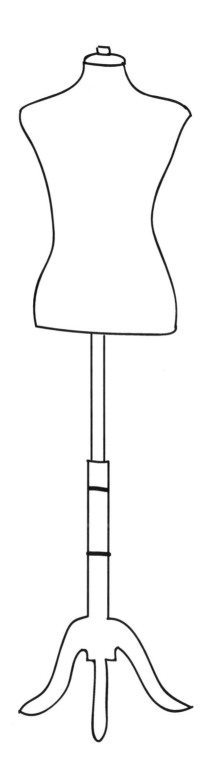

just a blank page waiting to be filled

My week in paper scraps!

- movie stubs
- receipts
- candy wrapper

Collect bits and pieces of evidence for a week stick it here

HOW Did you FEED your BRAIN!

Memories to

CHERISH

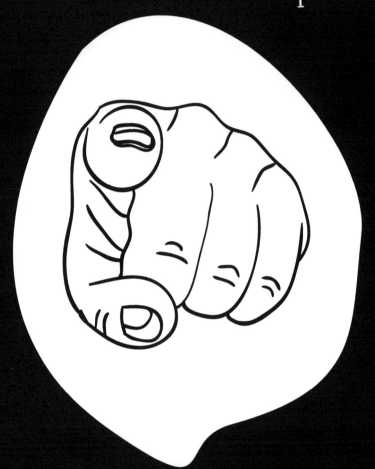

Spend today drawing everything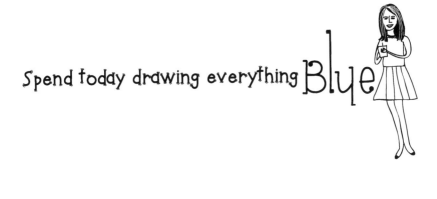

What does your future look like?

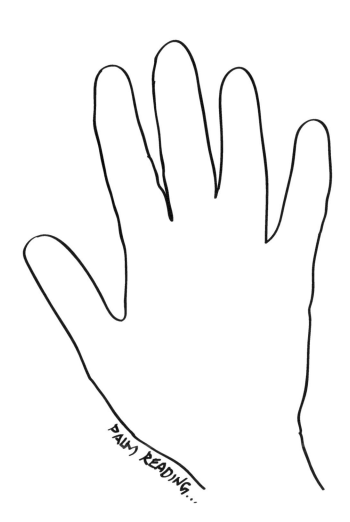

step 1 Create

step 2 Tear

step 3 Frame (optional)

step 4 Share it with someone

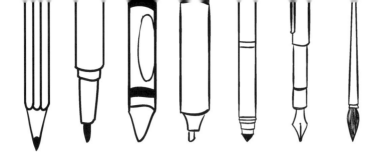

Experiment with different writing tools

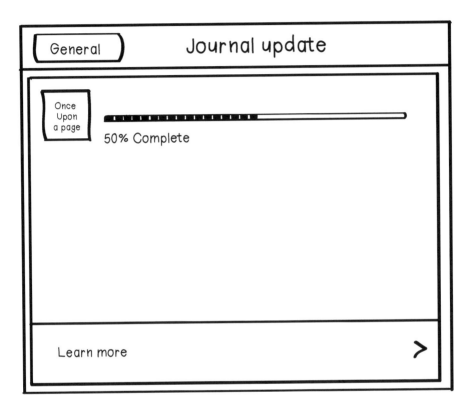

What is your inner chatter when
you want to take
a risk

SMEAR paint all over

watch the sunrise

Show your progress

Go through fashion magazines

Draw or place pictures of your style

In Style

tape an image you like

draw it on the opposite page

just one of those days

I'm feeling..

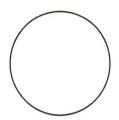

_____

I'm feeling..

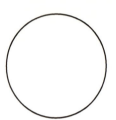

_____

I'm feeling..

_____

I'm feeling..

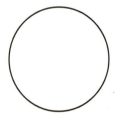

_____

I'm feeling..

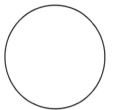

_____

I'm feeling..

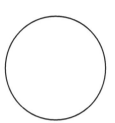

_____

SAY IT "I am...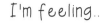

Strong Creative
Awesome Brave
Positive Kind
Go-Getter
admirable
Confident
Ambitious

Put pen to paper
don't worry
Just start a story...

All that Glitters..

Only shinny things on this page

The Page for

HIDE

the good you do, and

MAKE KNOWN

the good done to

YOU

(Ali ibn Talib)

write quotes that inspire you or create your own

Take your favorite book.

seal the pages

For my eyes only

What is the one secret you never told?

seal the pages

Page for
favourite

DECLUTTER

Draw all the things you

- Threw
- Donated
- Recycled

Your *Handwriting* is *unique* *different* and can *identify* you

Change it up!

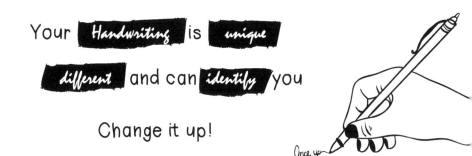

MONOCHROMATIC ART

calling all shades, tints and tones of one single color

Draw something from there

Fill a bag with goodies of all one color

Visit your local library.

Borrow books or magazines.

Call an old friend or a relative you haven't talked in a while

Summarize your conversation

_____
_____
_____
_____
_____
_____
_____
_____
_____
_____
_____
_____
_____
_____

COVER THIS PAGE WITH ~~coffee grinds, hair strands, candlewax~~, whatever you want..

Take a picture from an unusual angle

Observe and draw the road signs you see!

under the covers

make shadow images

STEPS TO A COIN PURSE

- Tear the page →

- Decorate it

- Fold along the lines

- Tape it to make a coin purse

- Put spare change through out the week

- When full give it to someone who needs it

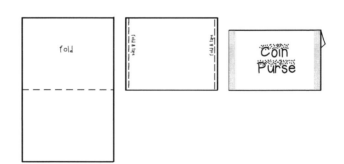

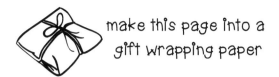
make this page into a gift wrapping paper

Take this journal for a walk

Pick leaves of all shapes and sizes

preserve it in this section

Declare your freedom

from that which

SHACKLES YOU

1. _____
2. _____
3. _____
4. _____
5. _____
6. _____
7. _____
8. _____
9. _____
10. _____

Scribble Dribble

Sow seeds

Draw the GROWTH

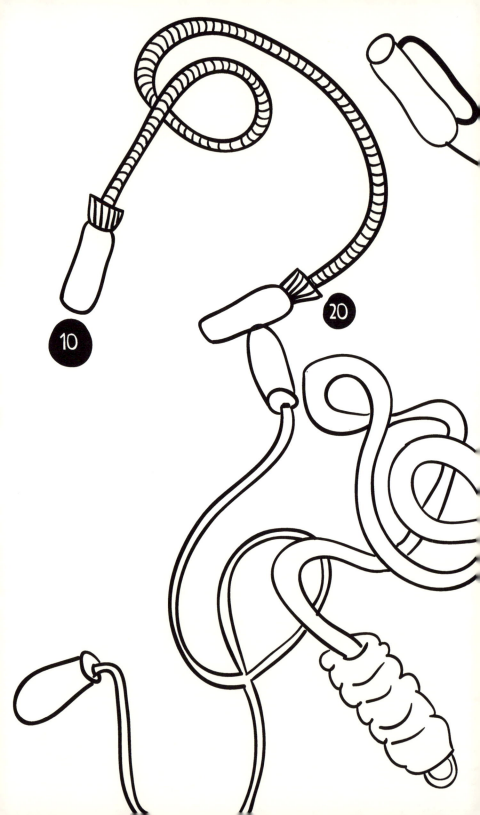

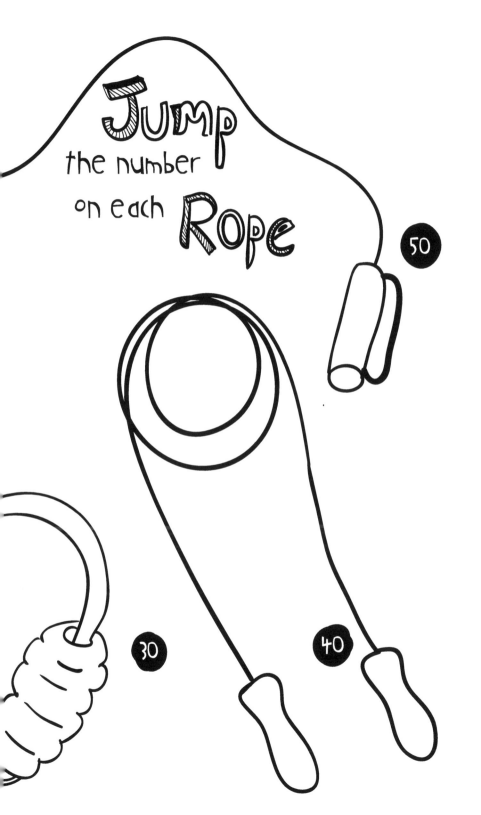

~~Think~~

COLOUR OUTSIDE THE BOX

YESTERDAY

TODAY

Make today better
than yesterday

Add pages to this page

DOT DOT DOT

draw images using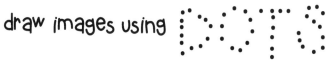

Face this page
AWAY from you
DRAW
an image

Stick a photo of your family or
a group of friends here.

point to each person and write something about them

PICNIC TIME

with you and this journal

WHO? are you OBSESSED with?

(yikes! Strong word.. Who do you admire and respect)

what are your inner  Demons

FACE THEM **CONFRONT THEM**

VISION

design your FUTURE

BOARD

Go after your desires

MEASURE

the thickness of
of this book AFTER
your creative work

_____ cm.

_____ inches

Made in the
USA
Columbia, SC